Pot O' Gold

Prose, Poetry and A Tale O' Thu' Sea

C.D. Hurley

PublishAmerica
Baltimore

First printing

ISBN: 1-4137-7908-5
PUBLISHED BY PUBLISHAMERICA, LLLP
www.publishamerica.com
Baltimore

Printed in the United States of America

Cover photograph courtesy of

KATHY TOTTEN

This book is dedicated to
MISS EMILY ELIZABETH McGAFFIGAN
and her wonderful friend,
CHLOE

Thanks to my friend and editor
"FREDDIE" TAPPAN

CONTENTS

TALES OF THE TRAIL

Cowboys have cows and jetboys have jets
but the trails demand the same needs.
Lonely starlit nights away from the ranch
cause some to fall in love with their steed.

Both carry a weapon for rattlers and such
but the good ones will never draw
on a tenderfoot or patsy, unless they git nasty
'n lodge in the poor fellows craw.

And jetpokes, as cowpokes, will never lie
'less it fits in the story, of course.
Best forget all his yarns, Dude, and dismiss all his tales
whether he's ridin' a jet or a horse.

WILD WEST

The earth rumbled as the mighty sound of a million buffalo or more
ran 'cross the prairie as if it were on fire, their spirit blended, one to all.
The heat of day mattered not and digging hooves on the prairie floor
made dust clouds so thick that none could hear or see where the weak would fall.

That's the way it was in the Wild, Wild West, where the red man lived each day
upon and off the land he loved in the deserts of an earlier time.
They searched for food that the land provided and the buffalo that they
had depended upon and had a reverence for and that brought them peace of mind.

Soon, the white man came upon their land just to kill the buffalo,
not for food or clothing or for any need except to take his land!
To take his land through the buffalo to which his livelihood was owed.
To eradicate the people called Indian, to eradicate the desert's red man.

His warriors fought against great odds to defend his own from this,
the ominous onslaught from invaders and their eradication threat.
Battles were won but more were lost and the end soon came, alas!
Then no more sounds of buffalo herds. Yes, no more needs were met.

"Oh! Great Spirit, Mighty Chief, who gave me all I have had,
what did I do to deserve this punishment from the invading white men?
Why did Your Spirits not help me; could my color have been so bad
as to put down my children and my grand-children's children,
cause us to meet our end?"

"Why did our love and reverence of Spirit not protect us from Your Wrath?
Why did You help the enemy of our wonderful life and land?
Oh! Great Spirit, I can only wait to find the answers in my quest
for a restful life of happiness and the love of my fellow man."

BEAVER BASH

There's mass destruction everywhere,
roads obstructed, here to there.
Devastated valleys and the streams are filled
since the beavers cut the trees on Temple Hill.

Cattle roaming the city streets,
ducks and chickens, where people meet.
Pigs at the restaurant eating their fill
since the beavers ate the fence-posts on Temple Hill.

Squirrels angry, chasing dogs around,
moose and bear have invaded the town.
Fish in the river 'cause the lake's all spilled
since the beavers let their dam go on Temple Hill.

Some folks say they struck at night,
the town went down without a fight.
The people are homeless but the animals are thrilled
since the beavers found a leak in grandpa's still,
on Temple Hill.

REFLECTIONS

As I gaze upon the beginning of winter's grip
I close my eyes and reflect on why God put me here.
Why on this spot? Why in this time?
Am I where He wants me? Have I lost perspective?
Should I reach out? Should I change my ways?

Did I take an easy trail instead of the path I should have trod?
Did I take the paved and worn footpath and easy bridges
instead of the shear challenge of cliffs where only eagles go?
When I gave my hand to man, did I feel his pain?
Did I feel the return of the love that I have loaned?

The love that I sowed and loaned to my friends who walked beside me
was the love that God and nature provided for me to give away.
Dare I hold hope of such sent back to fill my heart again
by those that I have befriended in my life or who has befriended me?
Have I earned it, earned it enough to be returned unto my soul?

I know I must provide for my own return of love from my fellow man.
I must sow love within myself for obeying Gods own words to me
of spreading seeds of love but to expect no harvest of my own.
My harvest comes from others sowing their crops of care for me,
for they will reap my love in their harvest as I have reaped their love for me.

Yes, falls fair warning gives us ample time, time to prepare
for winter's long cold grip.
I will harvest love from crops we were asked to sow in others in our spring.
Happiness will smile upon my face as that warm love is returned and stored within,
deep within the cribs of joy in my mind and soul.
And the love I have sowed will provide warmth and solace
for me all my winter through.

ODE TO MARIEANNE

Each time I see your gentle smile
I kiss you.
And when you softly touch my hand
I kiss you.
When our eyes meet across the room,
you whisper to me in soothing tones
or hold me close when we're alone
I kiss you.

When you listen to my day's trials
I kiss you.
When you hold me quietly when I am tired
I kiss you.
You prepare for me a welcome feast,
to boost my soul when I am weak
and when I limp home, you caress my feet.
I kiss you.

PALOMINO

"Which one o' you cowboys, this past Saturday night, took this old lady's
palomino horse?"
Thuh Marshal is askin' thuh questions n' us cowboys r' silent, o' course!
The old woman's a' sayin' that ahm thuh no good, pointin' straight
t' this ole cowpoke,
but I ain't a' sayin' it wuz me or it wuzzen't, that took her old nag as a joke.

So, I woke in thuh mornin' locked up in this jailhouse,
with the lowliest kind o' thieves
a' havin' a breakfast o' water, followed by a lunch o' beans.
I say, "Now wait one minute here, sheriff. I ain't thu one ye want."
He says, "Well, what ye say may be true enough, son, but yer sure the one I got!"

I tell the Sheriff, "Ole' Leroy done it, 'n' he should be thuh one that's here."
Then he tells me thuh old lady confessed t' that fact,
but Ole' Leroy is a' buyin' thuh beer.
While enjoyin' a warm red sunrise to a windy, frozen sky
in this flea-laden range-town jail in Texas, her Palomino goes a' gallopin' by.

COURAGEOUS LEADER

In a large mountain forest in Northern New Hampshire, a roaring mountain spring
repeats the ritual of springtime snow melt, as its travel to the ocean begins.
Across and around the rounded stones where trout will raise their young,
the white foamy bubbles now on their way, as a bear cub scrubs sleepiness away.

Quiet fills the forest this cool spring day as the doe lies panting in last year's grass,
in a spot under cover, away from the wind,
a soft wind that still carries winters chill.
Her time had come, her fawn would be born this day in April, this day in spring.
The herd had moved on, searching for food, moved on to the valley below.

And so did appear this tiny little deer, with mottled coat and long thin ears,
It stood in a minute and met the world under much inspection from the doe.
They smelled one another as she dried his fur and fed him and made him safe
by teaching him to lie in a death-still pose, a must-learn lesson in his new world.

And he did survive and soon was running with the herd's new citizens below
in the valley green, with grasses and flowers in the glen with the babbling brook.
And although there was order and discipline by mother,
they had plenty of time to play,
and the day was filled with races and jumping, growing bigger and growing wise.

A care free summer was shaping up, and he met his father so great and strong,
but his mother worried that many new bucks challenged his ability to lead.
As the great buck grew older, his body grew weaker from years of proving his skills.
His antlers were wide and scarred in his pride to defend his herd to his end.

It soon came to pass that the leader would meet a much younger and stronger buck
that battled him through daytime and nighttime. The noise was deafening.
The new buck prevailed and made it known that he was running the herd,
and the little deer's father did not return to the herd he had watched over for years.

But time moved on and the herd wintered in,
in a low spot on the east side of a mountain
and the little fawn grew and learned of the duties of the strongest and wisest of all.
He practiced learned skills against his playmates
and became accustomed to winning,
but in late winter, he found his first battle with a pack of hungry coyotes.

A snow-storm had started and the winds were noisy, and suddenly,
they were attacked.
The ruling buck was fighting his best but there were too many to stop.
The little fawn jumped to his feet over his mother and with the small antlers he had,
attacked them with frenzy, killing their leader and injuring many more.

The herd was proud to have a member so young to help defend their home,
and the ruling buck now let it be known that he had needed the young fawn's help.
They would walk together around the herd, looking for any other dangers.
The yearling fawn was so proud and happy to be trusted in this way.

As time passed, he grew and grew, and soon, he was long, tall and wide.
His mother was tiny now to him, and the herd leader was not as strong
as leaders should be to guard and guide and to battle intruders away.
And the fawn was no more, he was fully grown,
and he challenged his leader's hand.

It was certainly not a challenge to prove any point, just an urge that he suddenly felt,
a necessity to guard the herd and their home with the strongest and the best of all.
But the leader objected to his friend's advances, and a battle soon began
that lasted so long that when both were exhausted they would stop,
rest, then start again.

By sun-up, it was over. There was a new leader, this tall and handsome buck
He carried out his duties and showed merit and courage and soon,
the news was passed.
He was known through the valley,
and none would challenge this master or his bearing.
Even wolves and coyotes knew of this great one
and went to great measures to pass.

He watched over his herd and welcomed new fawns,
and their numbers grew and grew.
He was now the master of the largest herd and claiming mountain and valley below.
His walk to instill confidence by circling the herd was longer than ever before,
but he did so each evening
and again every morning and all the members knew him.

Soon, fall leaves were turning and an early snow falling
on this mid-September morning
The crisp air felt good as he walked through the forest,
then he noticed a different smell.
A strange smell! It stopped him! He sniffed and then saw it,
just a hundred yards away,
a hunters bright coat with a gun in his hand. He turned to warn his herd.

But a shot rang out and the big buck fell, his own blood filled his eyes.
In his pain and confusion, he arose to his feet and ran to his herd in alarm.
He warned them of the hunters and the dangers they faced
and sent them down the hill
to the valley below, the valley they loved; they had no time for plans.

The herd scattered out while running as fast as each one possibly could
trying to reach their place of safety, the place they had always called home.
He followed them now, knowing he was slower than he had ever been before,
then more shots rang out, and the great leader fell, never to lead again.

And later the herd, the herd he had led, walked on leaves left blood-soaked red
with no time to mourn his passing or no thought that a new leader is made.
Another buck will feel the urge to command, without even a word being said
and carry on this duty to his own kind, knowing respect's not given, but is earned.

Yes, today another buck will take his charge and gather all the does that he can.
An able young male will be temporary leader, as the herd's most responsible one.
He will get on with his duty and survive the winter,
then face a new challenge in spring
in selecting a responsible buck all over, the best leader for the herd.

OH, LIBERTY!

Oh, liberty! Your banner lies in state before me,
sacrificed solely for her precious youth.
Why have I been required to pay such a price to lose my blood, my soul?
I am as an oak leaf in the winter's cold wind that is caught in a fence-row, alone.
Yes, liberty! Your price is simply more than I think that I can pay.

Oh, liberty! Now, I must lay away the body in which my child's spirit resided,
God's heavenly gift that I have nurtured and taught and loved and now have lost.
The sting of death partakes of my rapture, and rips my heart from within me.
Yes, liberty! Your justice falls fair only to the un-assessed.

How will I best remember the payment that she made for me yes, for our freedom,
the payment that took her future from her, that we may live in peace?
I can't refuse this gift! I must accept, as it was left to all of us by my daughter.
Yes, liberty, I'll cherish her honor forever in all the people she left free.
Oh, God! Forever let her freedoms ring.

SERENDIPITY

No taste have I experienced,
no treasures have I owned,
no scenery have I ever viewed,
no words have I heard,
no music have I felt within,
no thoughts, from knowledge attained,
can match the sweet and lovely memories that I carry from my youth!

THE LAST LEAF

What's for certain, anyway?
The one thing I know is that I love you now, as I did then and more!
All my greatest love in times past is irrelevant today.
The words I used then seem so pale and inadequate now.
So, if my own past love is in question,
what's for certain, anyway?

My life's leaves are turning brown!
They had all the glowing colors of a rainbow then, and I didn't particularly notice,
so why do I notice now that they are all turned brown?
The approaching winter is starting to make this old oak's trunk cool, the sap to chill
but my love for you keeps my spirit forever warm.
'Till my last leaf is plucked by a cold north wind, I'll love you!

BIRTHLOVE

I was born into a great family and didn't know it then,
but what a wonderful gift of love it was that awaited me.
In my spiritual life, I'm promised an even greater Parent's love,
God's love; And that will last eternally!

JUST THOUGHTS

How can we know the meaning of the word "eternity" or the word "forever"?
Would "I will look for you in a few million years!" be complimentary in eternity?

None of the great and expensive varieties of gift-wrapping paper
that we have today,
however beautiful, excite my feelings like that simple
red and green paper we had when I
was a kid. I can remember white as the only other color,
and no child got white paper.

A circle, being encompassing, has no beginning or no end.
So, the only discernible point
is its center, and we must be there. Without it, there is nothing.
You and I, our Creator and
all His things must share this point of existence.

Why does my mind disobey me?
Why can't it let me live in a manner that I wouldn't
need to ask for forgiveness?

If given the chance, I would trade my life so that
my great-grandchildren could live as
free and happy as I, when I was a child.

You are the world! There is no life, except that which takes place within you.
Without your light, there would only be the void of darkness.

SNOWFLAKE

A snowflake was created in the heavens,
a place that is high in the sky
in the cool, cool blue of a high altitude
in a cloud of puffy white.

She was dressed in a gown of the whitest white,
and as her adventurous life began,
she floated and played among the heavens,
nurtured by gentle winds.

Millions of snowflakes played in the clouds
all patiently awaiting the day;
they would leave their home on an adventure
that would take them far, far away.

When mother nature called for them
to leave the place they were born,
many, many and many more flakes
stepped off their cloudy lawn.

The start of the trip was exciting,
and the joy of the journey was clear.
In quiet order they floated down, down and down,
a slow and soft ride through the air.

The little snowflake looked to meet others
and started to visit around,
making many new, lasting, friendships
as they floated toward the ground.

On, on and on they continued their trip,
gliding silently toward the earth.
She had noticed that 'though there were millions,
not one was exactly like her.

Closer, closer and closer they came
to the earth they had journeyed to meet
and in silence and order they softly landed
the first part of the trip was complete.

Then all the snowflakes joined petals as one,
to cover the land with their net,
to keep the young seedlings from being too cold
'till the spring suns kept them warm in their beds.

Then as the spring sun grew warmer,
the snowflake made her trip to the sea,
transformed to a drop of clear water
in a fast and ever-growing stream.

From a trickle, to a trout-brook, to a river
she traveled with the spring, to the sea
and floated in joy on ocean waters
to evaporate in the summer's warm breeze.

Then, one day she became airborne again,
and as she rode a warm suns ray,
she was gently placed on a plant by the rain
where she spent the summer at play.

Riding the streams and the rivers,
she was never, ever alone,
then at the end of a summer of play,
she rode another sunray home

Now, back in the heavens where she was born,
the snowflake floated around
and played in all of natures soft winds
with the friends that she had found.

Waiting for mother nature to call her
and direct her to begin
another trip to adventure, a trip to our earth,
to replenish our life again.

CLAUSTROPHOBIA

My temporary claustrophobic moments seem to have already lasted forever,
Drastically entombing my mind and body in some alien and virtually eternal prison.
I hear and see life suddenly from a terrible paralytic place with no future, only now!
I am bound a prisoner of instantaneous panic for what
always seems to last a lifetime.

On my escape, I lie in muted silence to collect and analyze my emotional feelings.
I understand my plight is based on some unknown and perhaps, groundless fear.
But that understanding does not change the torment that rages within me,
or calm the anguish of my claustrophobic mind.

THE ENLISTEE

I'm excited that I was accepted into the Army!
I don't have to plan, don't need one, I guess. Reality is just setting in.
I'm adventurously excited, yet worried because I don't know what to do.
I'm becoming scared and wonder why I enlisted. I'm sick in my stomach.
I already miss my family. Why did I do this? I feel like crying. I wish I hadn't!

At my new home, I'm met with terror, screaming and confusion,
nothing is familiar.
I'm kept running, working, new clothes, no sleep. I'm told that I'm a worm.
Finally, fall asleep and rudely awakened long before my body is rested.
Screaming and running. Even in the chow line they scream. Why?
Now living 18 inches from strangers I have a hard time understanding.

Scrub floors, latrines, doors and steps. If it doesn't grow, we paint it.
If it grows, we put rocks around it and paint the rocks, then move them.
No grass, sand everywhere, but not a grain can be on me,
not even on the soles of my shoes.
These clothes are too big, my shoes hurt. "What? What? I can't hear you!"
"I'm the best friend you'll ever have, probably the only one. Get your sorry
ass in gear, mama' s boy!"

"That snake you're sleeping beside is your brother.
Look at that poor excuse for a human."
"You had better make sure he listens and learns.
You'll depend on that mudball!"
"Do you hear me? What did you say, ladies?" "I asked you a question!"
"Get that smile off your face, mutton head. I do all the smiling here,
and I never smile."
"You want your mama, honey?
I'm you mama and your daddy. And I don't like you!"

"Straighten that line up; get that belly in. What's your name?
Are you sick, cry baby?"
"You look sick! You need to see the doc!
We're going to get shots and a haircut, honey!"
"Didn't I tell you all to shave before I saw your ugly faces?
You call that a shave, crud?"
"What did you shine those shoes with, an axe? Don't fall in again looking like this."
"You let a little thing like a shot bother you? You are slime!
Nothing but green slime!"

"We'll pick up every grain of sand on this base till
you find that cigarette butt I dropped."
"Look at this, two left feet. Do you have two left feet egghead? Shape up!"
"Pick it up: Hut-toop-threep-fourp. Looks like we'll be here this weekend, too."
"Worm, you're making us all look bad. Pick it up! You march like a cow!"

"I had better hear you!" "You hadda good home but you left" YOU'RE RIGHT!
"You wanna go back but you can't" YOU'RE RIGHT!
"Sound off" ONE TWOOP! "Sound off" THREE FOURP!
"Cadence count" ONE TWOOP THREEP FOURP, ONE TWOOP—
THREE FOURP!
"I didn't ask you to sing, mama' s babies. We are counting cadence here!"
"Whaddayou WACS? You sound like WACS! Are you a WAC Waco?" NO, SIR!
"Then sound off like soldiers, groundhogs! Let the ladies bridge club hear you!"
"We'll keep this up all day if we have to. Did I say keep quiet?" SIR, NO, SIR!
"Now sound off!" SIR, YES, SIR!
"Cadence count" ONE TWOOP THREEP FOURP—ONE TWOOP,
THREEP FOURP!
"Companaaaaaaaaay—Halt!" "Take ten! I have to go puke!"

"Don't lay that piece down, idiot!" "Did you learn anything from class?"
SIR, YES, SIR!
"Whaddaya think about this, meathead? You'll sleep with that weapon tonight, do you hear?" SIR, YES, SIR!
"Now, get away from me! Listen up! You have ten minutes to change into class 'B' uniform and fall in before me; do you understand me?" SIR, YES, SIR! "What did you say?" SIR! YES, SIR. "Platoon, attention! Now, fall out!"
"I better not find any beds wrinkled when I check!"
"Let's go! Let's go! you have six minutes left! Go, go, go!"

Marching for hours, the same thing, over and over again. "Platoon, atteeeention!" If I could just stop for a while, I could remember more! "Right shoulder, Ahms!" Now, I carry a piece or weapon. My life is centered on that weapon, I take it apart, I clean and oil it, I assemble it. I do it again and name all the parts. I must memorize the serial number. I must memorize all the General Orders, guard duty is an honor but I'm cold!

I make it to bed, I sleep for three hours and I'm rudely awakened to walk again. "Here's your orders, crud!" Orders? "Don't tell me you can't read, hillbilly?" Now, I am promoted and given a leader's position. "Well, now the captain has lost his watery mind. You a leader?"
"Git out of my face and take your squad of rejects with you."
"Git those lights out and shut up. Four AM comes early. I said shut-up!"

Classes, marching, shots, lectures where I can't stay awake, more and more. Saturday inspection. Worked most of Friday night to prepare.
Everyone fails anyway.
We wait, we wait and we wait! "Ateeeention!" Look straight ahead. Commander spends eternity checking my equipment. Returns to check again.
His assistant writes.
Leaves and returns. "Good job, soldier! Report to orderly room!" SIR, YES, SIR! What happened to Crud?" At least I knew my new name.

Report to First Sargeant. Handed three-day pass and told to eat first. After lunch, walking to bus stop. "Crud, wait, and I'll walk with you!" SIR, YES, SIR! "Where did you learn that crap, soldier? When I stoop so low as to talk to you, just say yes, sergeant, not all that other crap you've got in that little insect mind. Do you hear me, soldier?" SIR…er YES, SERGEANT! "Don't yell at me, Crud! Where we going?"

I feel like smiling for the first time in three months. "Git that grin off your poor excuse for a face soldier!" Got to write home, I feel good, I'm a soldier! Yep! I'm a soldier!

BUILDING A FAMILY LIFE

The soft warmth of a mother's breast is all that I now know.
Her voice so soft and sweet and gentle sings to me.
I know no hunger; Cold nor torment ne'er has touched my mind,
my emotions laid out for all the world to see.
I have been born as all before me, to a woman and a man.

I watch and learn as earnest siblings demonstrate for me
the way to move, to touch, to explore all of earths material things.
The wealth of family, home and friends are gently pressed within me
as life creates a boy from flesh and mind.
This boy, raised in family love and harmony.

My world consists of watchers, teachers and my friends to be
as mentors roll a carpet smooth before me.
Through principals, knowledge, needs and toils of labor,
I am molded into a citizen of their community
to earn a future of respect and love from all my fellow man.

I learn through stories, tales and facts that are passed down to me,
those acts expected of my life and my duties within this role.
By avoiding the wrath of any "ne'er-do-well," I come upon
who spreads by word of mouth or print, the heat from the fires of hell,
lest I lose connection to my Creator.

In youth, I yearn to see the land that may be hidden
just a short walk 'round the distant bend
and to throw off the chains that restrict the roaming in my happy heart.
Throw off the chains and venture over there to see;
yes, see and touch whatever's waiting there for me.

A smile is fixed upon my face, from joy residing deep inside me.
And lo! Another day before me breaks, in joyous light of dawn,
and then, another comes, as if it would never end.
Each day anew, each day another day of dreams, yes,
dreams that another soul left lying there for only me.

And just before adulthood came to me, at least in any form of mind,
I'm called upon to heed my country's call,
a call to arms, my duty, my gift to all mankind,
to render service to my country's will and need,
to offer my life to keep my country free.

I, in travel was exposed to other thoughts, from other minds of men,
who hailed from lands that had never been learned before by me.
I found an opportunity to expand my curious mind anew.
Another bend I had not known nor dreamed had ever waited there
in other's minds and other's words spoken in different tongues.

Another world to conquer! Another world to see and explore with you!
With your hand in mine, we start our journey to a place we could never dream.
As bold as any warriors ever were in war, we go our way unafraid,
to build a life of substance and responsibilities.
We will start and raise our family in love, together.

THE COUNTRY SINGER

While on this gig in North Kentucky,
I guess while I'm feeling lucky,
I'll try to put down somethin' I've wanted to talk about.
Just to somehow explain my feelins'
as to folks that are building ceilins'
to keep me in a room within "their house."

Well, now that ain't where I'm livin'
within your walls and lowered ceilins',
and maybe that's why I'm always runnin' away
to my "Freedom" kind of life
with my children and my wife
and to say whatever it is I need to say.

I was born, enjoyin' livin'
in this world of country singin',
and I take offense when some fool tries to say
that, "for him" I ain't livin' right,
singin' country every night.
But now, I don't enjoy them standin' in my way.

So, I load up my old van,
drive as far as I can,
stop and sing a few sad songs, and with some luck,
I can open a can of spam,
hereby known as "singer's ham"
then, enjoy a day of fun as a family man.

I don't pretend to tell you how
to plow your land or milk your cow,
so don't you tell me how to play my old guitar.
When I enter Tennessee,
I bow my head and bend my knee.
Here a man is blessed by "country," wide and far.

But now, that ain't the only thing
this great state is proud to bring
to get folks to rockin' in their shoes.
You can mosey down to Memphis
grab a chair and beer and join us.
Just sit down on old Beal Street to a meal of blues.

From Old Virginia west to the river,
from Missouri to the Carolinas,
and all that beautiful country in between,
five hundred miles of Tennessee State.
When I leave, I just can't wait
to return to where a free man ought to be.

Yea! I'm speakin' 'bout the great State of Tennessee!

HUNTER AND PREY

The rider sat lumped and as still as a stone upon his saddle-less mount,
gazing into the valley below, looking for the slightest move
that would give away the hunters' positions, their advantage to reveal
to the hunted, in this game of life and death,
to the hunted, the enemy's quest.

Many moments he sat and stared below at the soft forest floor
with little caution he slid from his steed and fell upon the ground.
He crawled in pain to the babbling brook and began to wash his wounds
in a desperate attempt to live for his duty,
for his duty to his tribe.

He awakened with a start and realized that he had fainted from the shock
from the cold water which covered his wounds and chilled his burning blood.
His pony stood still and waited for his rider to mount again
and to ride on to the red man's campsite
where the sweet, cool grasses are.

A few moments of rest and, although in pain, the warrior rode away
being careful to avoid any open land or suspected travel paths.
Slowly down the windswept hills where he hunted as a boy,
sitting easy on his loyal pony,
his pony that was taking him home.

At dusk, their trip ended when they came to the village
where the tribal leaders meet,
and campfires were glowing and the chanting and dancing had already begun.
Tribe leaders were eating and discussing their problems as
our battered warrior rode in,
still showing many wounds of the battle,
still bleeding from his wounds.

He had been on a hunt to a distant mountain, and the
horse-soldiers were waiting there
to ambush the hunters; their plan had succeeded, he had left many wounded men.
He had ridden his pony deep into the forest and as high as they could climb
to escape from the many horse-soldiers,
to return to his tribe with the news.

The leaders had meetings, the warriors prepared, and he and his pony were fed.
His wounds were attended, his war chest was opened, and he made ready again
to find the horse-soldiers and rescue the hunters, whom he had left behind.
To find the horse-soldiers and rescue the hunters,
that must be the war party's mind.

Soon after the war-talk, the party departed for the day-long and demanding ride
past the place where he had hidden, and then on to the hunter's camp.
Hiding their ponies and setting afoot, soon, they were very near.
They rested and readied their weapons.
They prepared to rescue their friends.

Then, after dark, when things were quiet, they circled the soldiers' camp,
and with a whippoorwill call, they attacked as one, surprising the sleeping force.
After a long, vicious battle and as night finally ended, the fighting quieted down.
Now, he tried to count the warriors,
tried his successes to weigh.

Our warrior gave the call of the whippoorwill and waited but no answer came.
He waited a while and called out the names, no answer came again.
He left his rock fortress and moved quietly through the bodies
with his eyes working hard
to find someone he had rescued
but not a live warrior was found.

He moved silently past the horse-soldiers' campfires, with bodies everywhere
both red men and white were lying still but he finally saw someone move.
As he turned to find if it was friend or foe a loud and white flash exploded.
and that is the end of our story
that's as far as our story goes.

LOVE ME

If I held your hand in mine,
would you love me?
If I held you in my arms,
would you love me?
If I looked into your eyes and invited you to paradise,
would you accept me in your life?
Would you love me?

You could lift me into heaven
if you loved me.
I would want to live forever
if you loved me.
I could sing to you my songs of love and with the help of God above,
sail through life, as on the wings of doves
if you loved me.

UNPUBLISHED

Years of history went unpublished, yet clearly understood,
when the stooped and age'd lady clasped the cold,
callused hands in the coffin
for the last time
and tears of love and sorrow mixed, dropped freely on a new blue suit.

SHIMMERING WATERS

Lo! The morning sun stands full, a flaming conglomerate of fire,
and commands respect from all that sees its power of making shadows meek.
In my early days, I wouldn't have watched the clouds abscond or the fog dissolve,
but now, acknowledging his domain, I bow to him. As king, he reigns!

While wolves allow their prey to graze for future feasts for their forays,
an eagle soars in silent flight to complete its mission before the night.
Suns dimming warns that dark is nigh; the curtain draws, a coyote cries.
Then, evening comes and quickly fades to herald the end of this winter's day.

A time of silence follows the light. The stage is set. All wait for night.
The hunter's moon reflects the sun, too light to hide, too bright to run.
The shadows, heavy with their guests, allowing refuge or a much needed rest,
in a continuous game of hide and seek, of life and death for the slow or weak.

Off in the distant mountain heights, in unison, the wolf pack cries.
Their psychological war has begun, committing some to silence, some to run.
The quiet of the forest returns again, and the search for food and water begins.
Soon, the wolf's dread song is lost to need, and the forest dwellers drink and feed.

Bright moonlight is reflected far below in a shimmering stream in the valley floor.
Through the outstretched limbs of lowland trees, the water creates an eerie scene.
Now, in silent movement along its banks, the wolf-pack "closes in" its ranks.
With adjusted gait to their hunting speed, they look for food to fulfill their needs.

In an opening, scarce a mile away, a deer herd grazes on winter hay,
trying to keep their body sound with the precious little grasses found.
The wolves pair off, two and two, and now, the pack begins pursuit.
Each one has individually found their place and cadence without a sound.

Soon, the wolves have taken their place and wait for the signal to start the race
for survival of either wolf or prey. Nature shows favor neither way!
As though on a starter's signal gun, the wolves attack the herd as one.
A precision team; the plan is done by culling out and isolating one.

And then, the kill with a "coup de grace" the herd falls silent, while others watch
their comrade make the sacrifice. Most are winners, but one paid the price.
Tomorrow, another game begins, and skill will determine who will win
in this game of life, of life and death, but now, for the moment at least, all rest.

I NEED TO LIVE AGAIN

I need to live my life again to rectify all my wrongs.
I need more time to listen
to all of life's sweet songs.

I need to demonstrate to the world that we can all get along.
Because I learned these things too late in my life,
I need to live twice as long.

THE SPIRIT OF THE RED SOX FANS

The Red Sox played another ho-hum season
always second as autumn begins,
losing long and futile battles
will the '04 season never end?

Only a wild-card space exists now.
Playoff games with the Yankees begin.
Then the Sox prolong the misery,
just one more loss and the season ends.

Spirits soared as on wings of eagles,
smiles from hope that "the curse" has passed.
A win today and a dream for tomorrow
The Red Sox win one more, at last.

Saw fans crying, bats start booming
slamming baseballs into the stands.
Ortiz, Manny, even Damon
starts batting thunder once again.

Arroyo, Pedro, Wakefield, Schilling,
It mattered not who was on the mound.
All of them became pitchers, perfect!
The winning spirit came to Boston town.

Game after game, the Sox begin winning.
No team has ever done this before,
but when the American league playoffs are over,
the mighty Yankees are mighty no more.

On to meet our National League challengers.
The Cardinals welcome us to their town,
but the Red Sox spirit proved too strong now.
The Red Sox easily put them down.

Red Sox fans and the team, together
created an unbeatable force,
to bring a team from loss to victory
The Boston Red Sox Team, of course.

UK

There was once the time of a man named Uk
who often wondered how He could to make a buck
'cause nothing had been invented yet to sell,
and he lived in a cave-house, anyway!

He tried "stock broker" but there were no stocks to buy,
tried "onion seller" but only made his-self cry,
tried "bus driver" but had no wheels
nor routes to travel yet, anyway.

He tried "fisherman" but that made him scream
because all kinds of things crawled out of the stream.
There was cows and dogs and even man evolving,
gettin' overcrowded here, anyway!

He tried being "President" but didn't have a senate;
he formed a government but no one was in it.
So, he settled on "inventor" but "what do I invent?
and what would you use it for, anyway?"

Then, he became a "pizza-man" but had no cheese
because cows were then learning how to climb trees.
He mixed up some ingredients and left them in the stump,
lightning hadn't brought him fire yet, anyway!

So our friend lost faith in winning the rat race,
lost confidence in preparing a "professional" place
for his-self or a wife if he could ever catch one.
He would never have enough stone treasures, anyway

So, he threw all his possessions in his hollow log
and wrote a letter to Klug, willing him his dog.
Having no chance in the commercial world,
Uk decided to end it all, anyway!

He was tired of even trying to get ahead,
so he settled on suicide and speared his-self's head.
When Klug found his leavings, he proudly said,
"Uk's stump has turned into Sliced Sunbeam White Bread!"

SNOWSTORM

Something happens when awaiting snowstorms
that bring a quiet anxiousness to my mind
and stops the race of life that's always happening
within the world of all it will involve.
Perhaps the knowledge that indeed, there's something
that surpasses all the power we know exists
with it's silence starting oh, so slow and gently,
closing off all vision, sounds and feel.

Quietly falling, touching light upon my skin
and painting all the world in cleanest white.
Hemlock branches bowing down to meet her,
to surrender their great stature to her might.
Deeper, deeper and more silent she becomes now,
all move slower as her silence stills the land
with purity spread o'er all the earths possessions,
recalling thoughts from the treasures of my mind.

My solitary thoughts now dwell within me
in close proximity to that which I can see,
as if to guide me in my process of thinking
of my life's true worth and my philosophy.
My mind wanders through my former years now,
calling on my memories within this time.
My circle is closed to outside intervention.
Just me, my God and the white of snows that fall.

I walk alone in blind anticipation
of what I'll see when the warm sunshine returns
with that great reward that always follows snowstorms
of a glory-land, the birth of the world again.
Sunshine follows her snows with greater brilliance,
reflecting sight and mind to a bluer sky.
My footsteps squeak and frost forms on my breathing
as if she left an obstacle in trade.

I stop as I see in the horizon,
my boyhood from a higher plane;
I see my parents and I see my siblings
and the home in which it all began.
I find this precious part of life a welcome
to which neither time nor date can lay their claim,
and life is stilled in retrospect with memories
recalling that ancient youth of mine.

A glorious time of love and peace remembered
of the beauty, grace and times of a life that's passed,
where skies were blue and golden sunsets beckoned
all my worries and my restlessness away.
Old thoughts and visions now return to me
while the things I hold and held forever dear
bring smiles and a lightness to my humble heart
waking feelings carried deep within my soul.

I always find the gentle breezes flowing there
o'er greenest grasses of the springs gone by
rustling leaves of recollection, blowing oh-so-softly
and replenishing my cache of life from then to now.
Then, I return to all my life's realities
as the snow's sharp winds erase my peaceful dreams,
but I'll remember the snowstorm's transformation of my mind,
and I'll dream my memories over when I sleep.

THU WEDDIN'

Lydia looked suh good in pank, sheed bin a' workin' in thu sun.
Luke 'ud come t' claim her as 'is be-trothin' one.
Ma was grinnin' nice n' wide, showin' er' borroy'd teeth.
Lil' Sis wuz a-walkin' slow in front, a' carryin' a corn husk wreath.

I walked over t' see if I could sooth muh poor Pa' s old shattered heart
fer today 'iz furst-borned daughter wuz a-planning t' depart.
"She could plow a row, straight as a man," he 'ud say, "her n' 'at old mule."
(He 'ud allus let 'er finish thu field a' fore uh sendin' 'r off t' school.).

Thu tears wuz a-runnin' down 'iz cheeks n' ye cud' see 'iz heart were broke.
He choked back on 'iz chaw n' spit at uh target (uh piece o' rotted rope),
so I said "Don't worry, Pa, lil' Sis an' Ma can do thu plowin', you'll see!"
"Oh! At's not whut Ay'm a-cryin' fer, son. Ma' s shoes are jes' a' killin' me!"

LOST LOVE

The loudest sound is the sound of silence
where a child, gone to heaven,
once played.

The deepest loss is the loss of someone
that we believe
we can't endure.

I hear the soft, sweet songs of memories
you left playing
in my soul.

You took all life's good things
when you left me, my love.
Yes, all good things, but those.

MEMORIES OF A LADY

In the clear, crisp break of an autumn dawn,
a brand new day I see
awaiting me.
My mind uncluttered, my thoughts are clear,
and in silent bliss, I drink in the start
of this new day.

I stand, inhaling the brisk of the mornings welcome.
Cold air takes life-giving breath
deep inside me.
My body, mind and soul all meld together,
providing life's manna for me,
a place for my spirit.

Through the window, I see the ocean's waves.
In her beauty, her strength,
I hear her call.
I walk upon warm sands that hold a million memories.
Each grain, individual and different,
each one with a tale.

I feel the salt air breeze, warm upon my face
and smile with pleasant memories
of days now gone.
"Never-ending" times that ended all too soon
still bring a smile, with sadness
as I know they're gone.

I hear a gull's shrill scream and, before me, see a lady
in flowing clothes, walking straight to me
and calling my name.
A look so familiar to my forgetful mind;
old scenes, racing deep into my soul.
I see my only love!

How can this be my love, my love that died too soon?
Mind and vision pair to torment me.
She now comes near.
"May I walk with you?" she asked and took my hand in hers.
In silence, I cried, "What is happening to me?"
She stopped and smiled.

"I am manifest' of our love. I'll stay until you awake!
I'll walk with you, then I'll go back home
to wait for you."
"I will never awake!" "But oh, you must! Live your life to its end!
My spirit is with you, wherever you go,
as on the day we wed."

Touching my lips with the breeze she wore,
she whirled around me and faded away,
my lady love.
Now, in the clear, crisp break of an Autumn dawn
a brand new day I see,
awaiting me.

TREASURES OF MOTHER NATURE

As a tiller of the soil and navigator of the earth, sea and air,
I have lifted up my eyes to the wonders of the majesty in one shining grain of sand,
and I have looked down on cathedral peaks that architects could never duplicate.

Projecting my niche in neither place,
I'll try to live among their statures and justify mine.
I behold these treasures with a tinge of guilt for invading their holy alters with my sight,
and gazing upon their most private solitudes, solitudes they inherited from our Creative God.

Oh, mother nature! Surely, Heaven can offer little more than this.

NIGHTTIME CONFUSION

I sometimes wake up in the middle of the night
when everything suddenly, is either "black or white."

I wonder why I said what I said when I said it.
I attempt to light a candle and find I've already lit it!

I rush because my actions just can't wait until dawn
then wake up when I pull my ice-cold boots on.

It's then that I realize that I'm not quiet awake
and I know full well, now, that I am making a mistake.

Then, I think, "I can get some more sleep anyway!"
And tomorrow, I'll re-emphasize what I said today!

AROUND THE BEND

Around the bend in front of me there lies a special place,
a place that we all want to get to, a place with all good men,
where all is fair, and smiles are free from all the folks who live there.
But it seems just a little further, each time we round the bend.

I've never met a person in my life that wouldn't like to go there,
to this place we all could live in, a place we could all call home
where we treat each other equally and live in peace and harmony.
But it seems just a little further, each time we round the bend.

What happens to us as we walk the road to this place that we hear is so near?
What change takes place within us along this straight part of the trail,
that causes us to lose the desire to live our lives with others?
Then, it seems a little further, each time we round the bend.

Someday, I hope my children will find the passage as it was meant to be
and live in joy and peacefulness with all their fellow men.
What a wonderful thing, and it is there for free, if they will only take it.
Yes, life could be so wonderful, just around the bend.

THE SILENT BELL

Try as I may, I can't recall the first glimpse I got of this creature.
In my young mind, there always was this girl, this small and precious thing
with silvery-blond hair and soft sweet voice and tiny little features.
I accepted her looks and sounds as hers, as I did with any other beings.

She was nothing special, nothing grand and nothing special to see.
Just a sister that loved and was loved by the family, and I knew that she loved me.
My baby sister, like the others, just was and would always be.
We grew up together, played together and shared our company.

There were no big moments, no special feats, or monumental flukes
that marked our friendship from any other, even if we could have seen.
We grew together, not questioning fate and accomplished the few little duties
that parents and siblings laid out for us, duties that a family brings.

I respected her differences as she did mine and each gave the other space
to act as demonstrated by our siblings or to be as we felt so, the need.
I expected lady-like things of her, and she stayed well in her place
and treated me as a loving brother. She always had a smile for me.

But I left her when ordered to duty for my country, to answer the call of my peers
to military duties, whatever they would be and wherever I was to be sent.
I was gone for many a month on end, that turned into many a year.
I missed my family, my sister, my friend in my deep and recurring lament.

She was married and traveled all over the world while I married and settled down
a thousand miles from the home we shared, a thousand miles from family.
I saw her next when she was thirty-three, and both our lives had found
another to share our lives and our home, another one to share our ramblings.

Oh, we talked and we laughed and reminisced some and enjoyed each others spouse.
We explained our work, our new career and cares within our lives.
But then, when that visit was over, we returned to another house
not shared with our parents and siblings, yet not parted from old family ties.

Our families went on living and working, as we each saw fit to do.
We seldom returned at coordinated times so I wouldn't see her again
until our children were raised, attended school and then so very soon,
were themselves married and family traditions, for new families, would begin.

Oh, I called her, and she would call me, whenever we got around
to taking some time from a busy schedule that we all are trained to keep.
And every few years, we would see each other as both wound up in town
in a coincidental schedule or circumstance that happened to cause us to meet.

Then, in her retirement she moved back home, so again we would meet and talk
about old times and the places we'd been and how separation wouldn't be repeated.
We promised each other that once a year we would meet and maybe take a walk.
We would talk and laugh, as we did as kids, and for years our plan succeeded.

She sent me a bell to hang on my wall and promised to ring it someday
when she came to visit during her vacation, at the next start of summer weather.
I hung it and waited and smiled when I saw it because soon,
she would be on her way,
and we could re-live all our good times and have both our families together.

We laughed and joked and enjoyed ourselves, and I brought up her trip coming later
but our conversation was interrupted, as she told me that something was wrong.
She had found she had cancer and limited time, and it was a difficult measure
to take her mind from her greatest worry that she would leave her children alone.

A short ten months later, she went on to heaven, and someday, I'll meet her there.
We'll talk and laugh and walk some more, and no worry will ever dwell.
She'll again meet her children,
and I'll meet mine, and our families will forever share
the joys of eternity, of bliss and great happiness, and for the first time,
I'll hear her bell.

LAST WISH

Where daffodils are called Easter flowers and summers last forever,
is the very place where I long to be.
Where I can hear laughter with music and happy songs
and all those, that I love, are with me.

Where worry is a word, never thought of nor heard,
and all life's necessities are free.
If you will take me back home, I'll never more roam.
It's the last place I ever want to be.

THE WIND LION

On a warm sunny day, a gentle breeze blows through the meadow
and wafts the leaves.
The wind feels good upon my skin and lifts my spirits high and clean.
And if I listen to the song, I feel its touch as its sarong
is wrapped around my soul and mind with a soothing message of "resting time!"

Then, in the fall, when change is due, the winds sweep the land as clean as new.
The leaves are plucked; the trees stand bare.
The fields are cleared with freshened air.
The start of fall is warm and quiet but fall meets winter with all its might.
The direction changes from all around to mostly northerly with a howling sound.

Winter winds are vicious with their cutting chill,
but the white snow falls so softly still.
It seems a truce is wedged between the gentleness of snow
and a wind that's so mean.
When the snowfall ceases and the nights are long, it serenades us with frozen song.
The sounds of winter, a haunting cry, like sounds of a werewolf waiting nearby.

But the signs of spring will soon be here, signaling the start of a brand new year.
Though the wind will rest when the air is warm,
compared to winters heavy, wet storms,
we're reminded often of what's to come when February's fickle month is gone.
Leaving March with a departing roar, until next winter, the lion is no more.

WHY

Why can't we be as we were then, in the days when we first met?
As I did my chores, I couldn't see more than the world within your face.
Then, I realized I was completely in love and other things were well, just that!
And I wanted nothing more than to have assurance that you also wanted me.

Why can't it be as it was then, when you needed nothing more
than a blue-eyed clown with no gold in store and no budget to work around?
Then, the future meant nothing except being with you and having you to love me.
I was blind to all others, nothing else mattered, just then, forever and you.

Why can't life be as life was then, why argue, sit alone or cry?
I know that I love you but don't tell you as often as I did when we were kids,
and you never hold me any more, sitting silent for hours on end.
We are nice, yes, we're nice to each other, but we now live our lives as friends.

Where is it now? When did it leave us? Why didn't I see it go?
Now, old and slow and reliving my memories, I'm bending down with age.
Oh, what I would give to live our love over, to have you still loving me,
as when I first asked, "What's your name, pretty lady?"
and "Could I see you again?"

Can we do it again, is the light still there? Are the coals still warm from the fire?
Would you smile again if I asked for a date? Would you hold me once again?
Are the coals extinguished? Are the embers still there? Is the fire in you gone cold?
Are there memories there to ignite the spark to keep me eternally warm?

Why can't we be like we were then, when we were young, bold and in love?
Why can't we have just one more day when we each want the other's self,
and you care for me, and I care for you before it becomes too late?
I'll cry when I lose you and you will me, so come, let's be that way again.

THE SPIRIT INSIDE

I wonder what that spirit is that is looking through these eyes of mine,
and who that is that's been making use of the thinking part of my brain?
Was it thinking my thoughts as it used my hands for its own questionable deeds?

Has it invaded my heart? I wonder what it thinks of the love I carry down deep inside!
Does it acknowledge my views or even know of the ones
that has meant so much to me?
Could it know of my broken hearts or the loves that I knew that caused them to be?

Can I not stop this consciousness that controls my fate in spite of me
and takes my mind to places where I myself, would never dare to tread?
I sometimes am afraid to follow there, even as I know I eventually must,
and yes, I will!

Do I dare not ask it's name? Does it not know, nor care what name is mine?
Shall I tempt our association to disorder by demanding
that it stop its actions or go away?
What purpose does it wish to accomplish with me, if indeed a true purpose exists?

Is there not another consciousness there at all? Is it a conjecture of my own mind?
Do I try to ignore the things I know that must be done
and must be done by me alone?
Am I trying to deny the basis of my character by a creation of my own imagination?

I want to clear my mind of the things that I no more, want to bear within myself
and try to stop my thoughts of things that I do not want again, to think about.
Yet, who is this voice inside me now that demands these things I should do?

What is this spirit that is looking through these eyes of mine?
Does it see the way I do? Is it an agent of my soul or simply an influence over it?
What does my spirit demand in my life? What do I demand of my spirit,
indeed, what do I demand of me?

TORTURE OF THE INNOCENTS

From the United States Army, no rescue comes,
no rifle shots, no exploding bombs,
no jet-plane sounds and no green berets.
Abandonment shows upon his face.

Agony covers his face in frowns
with tears of torment streaming down.
No camaraderie and no way to go home,
a captor's mercy will not be shown

As greater wrath is brought to bear
the free world has shown little care.
Abandoned now by his very best friends
and shackled before his escape could begin.

Deprived of freedom's guarantees,
crying out for mercy on bended knees,
he pleads for the world to understand
he is just a young innocent man

The clock strikes six, the time has come.
There is no refuge no reprieve is won,
no prayers are said to relieve his fear.
There is no one to argue, no one to hear.

Now, the enemy states a few terse words,
then agonizing cries of pain can be heard.
Incarcerated and tormented against his will.
Our baby son finally swallows his pill.

WASTED MILLIONS

A million years since you've been gone and millions of
miles between me and you.
words I should have said.
plans that were never made.
chances I didn't take.
apologies I didn't make.
days I walked alone.
whispers I didn't hear.
dreams I dreamed alone.
thoughts I had of you.
moments we didn't share.
touches I never felt.
memories we didn't make.
people, but I'm so alone.
looks I should have seen.
kisses that should have been mine.
smiles I never saw.
stories we didn't tell
hands, but none were yours.
arms, but none reached for me.
nights I longed for you.
and now, in the autumn of my life, please know that I love you still!

The Purple Sharks

"LAAADEEEZE AND GENTLEMEN! WELCOME TO JOPPA FLATS AND TO THE 10,000TH PERFORMANCE OF THE PURPLE SHARKS PRECISION SAIL DEMONSTRATION TEAM"

The good ship *Nickelodean* was tugging gently on her mooring on this bright and breezy day. It's a nice day to get some ocean air and tidy-up the cabin. Vents are opened, jackets stored and things are made ship-shape after a week of sailing. "Messin' 'round" has begun! Soon, both cockpit bench seats are occupied with horizontal bodies, and lazy conversation has replaced the chore-minding.

"What did you do over the weekend, Grandpa?" the granddaughter asked.

"Went down to Massachusetts to watch the Blue Angels Flight Demonstration team. Did I ever tell you 'bout the Purple Sharks Sail Demonstration team?"

"No! What's that?"

"Well, six of the most beautiful red, white and blue sailboats were lined up in front of the American Yacht Club. Large gold numbers, indicating their assigned positions, were displayed on their bows. People crowded the shores of Joppa Flats for miles when sails were raised precisely at 1:00 p.m., and the first four boats departed the area in perfect alignment. Their hulls glistened with paint that is renewed after every show. They quickly disappeared up the river while the two remaining boats dropped their mooring lines at exactly the same instant. While accelerating toward the crowd, they turned to opposite directions at the last moment, spraying the screaming spectators with the cool waters of the Merrimack. They continued traveling on opposite courses, getting smaller and smaller 'til they disappeared from view.

"Suddenly, people began pointing toward the bridge where two of the team of four boats were speeding on a full downwind run, toward the starting point. No! There are four boats, still in tight formation, but the lead and trail boats are inverted, their keels pointing straight up. As they crossed the starting point, the inverted boats completely submerged while the remaining two fish-tailed away from the spectators. Meanwhile, numbers five and six are quickly returning from opposite directions with full sails and on a perfect collision course. Their wakes spouted foamy waters high in the air and at the last second before impact, they suddenly dived into the depths, leaving only a noiseless ripple as witness to their existence.

"Would you roll a can of that Diet Coke over to me darling? Thanks, love!

"Now, numbers one through four had returned, demonstrating slow sailing, dangling their dock lines from the left side of their bows, creating hardly a disturbance in the water. Amid 'Oohs' and 'Ahhs,' they quickly accelerated to unbelievable speeds while accomplishing a full 180 degree turn and simultaneously changing from a side by side to an in-trail formation as they sped away. Hold on! One sailboat is approaching from the bridge…no, there's two, but one is inverted! His keel is barely breaking water alongside number five's port side. The crowd applauds wildly as they pass at full speed, leaving an incredible wake in their path.

"Then, for what seemed an eternity, the spectators searched the waters for signs of the team. Someone would say they saw something, and another would say they thought it a gull or a seal. They waited and waited…then! Like a shot, all six boats surfaced in perfect unison and formation. With their bows pointed toward the heavens, they thrust their chocks into their mooring lines then swung to face the crowd, creating an enormous white-capped wave. The show was over! The 10,000th Purple Sharks Precision Sail Demonstration Team show was completed! The pilots sat on the bow of their boats and signed autographs for every spectator who wanted to swim out to get one."

"You really expect me to believe that, Grandpa?"

"Well, no girl! You should know that Joppa Flats is not deep enough for a Purple Sharks demonstration."

An Old Sailor's Last Ride

"Meditation and the sea are wedded forever!"
Herman Melville, novelist

NOTE:

My granddaughter mentioned to her university English professor, who edited a maritime magazine, that her grandfather wrote sailing articles. They found that her grandfather had published sailing stories in the professor's magazine. Through her, he asked me to write a paper about my age and its effect on my sailing abilities.

My story, "An Old Sailor's Last Ride!" began as an earnest answer to that request. However, after writing of my life's philosophies and the problems that I had just began to encounter, I found that I had left no path to a "closure" of that article as I had not "finished." I was still very much alive, indeed, and that fact begot fiction and an "old salt," by the name of Bones. The story is true to that point. I loved researching his 1700s dialect and pirate history, especially because I sail around the Isles of Shoals. The professor wanted no part of fiction. Too bad! I'm glad I met "Bones."

C.D. Hurley

Chapter One

We had enjoyed a great noon meal at Michael's Harborside Restaurant in Newburyport, Massachusetts, and were taking a walk through the Windward Yacht Yard. While watching the workers retrieval of a sailboat from the Merrimack River, Granddaughter picked up an old yellowed piece of line.

"What kind of line is this Grandpa?" she asked, adding, "It looks weird!"

"Hmm. It does look different, doesn't it?" I replied. "Probably fell off an old pirate ship that Butch had to repair and it had to make a fast getaway!"

Granddaughter took another look and smiled, then placed the old string into her pocket for future study.

I have always loved a walk in a boatyard, even when all the boats are not here. Replaced parts and equipment still lie around amid paint cans and boat stands. Some of the boats are left in the yard for various reasons. Owners have moved and left their boats in the care of the professionals or are on vacation, or as I have to face soon, the sailor got too old to sail. Each boat has a different story to tell. It seems as if they can tell their story sometimes by their very appearance. Here, boats that show neglect share a home with yachts that get the best of care. There is no better place to see why we give the yacht name to a boat that is used for pleasure. Ugly work-boats are parked right alongside sleek racing yachts and corporate showpieces. Some show a sign that they are for sale. The sign may as well say, "You were beautiful when I bought you at the boat show, but now, I had rather have the money!" But I think the boat may be thinking, "My feeble owner can't sail me for another season!" I laugh, but my thoughts turn to myself. I am getting older and slower. My back and knees are healed but weak. I think, *How much longer can I sail with the safety that I demand of my sail-mates?*

I am sure that *Nickelodean*, my motor-sailor, has had her thoughts on the subject. As I get older, I admit that I have a few inattentive muscles that occasionally punish me with a jab of pain, just for asking them for assistance. I also notice that I take fewer chances, though each year I have less life to lose in failure. Maybe it is self-preservation, which is no sin, or maybe I am avoiding the embarrassment of failure. In any case, I've noticed recently that I had really rather sail with someone who has some sailing skills first, with the social skills of conversation second: in other words, a quiet helper. My need for friends is outweighed by my need for quiet solitude that I have found only in the mountains where I was raised, the sky that I fly or the sea that I love. I have also learned that their solitude can be interrupted by often-good intentions.

Sometimes, I drive my aged convertible automobile to the river park or sit alone on my boat for hours, reflecting and enjoying the moments alone. My boat invites me to be free and to sail away with her. I wrote the following poem for those times.

"Tack" to windward, "run" to lee
and take me, *Nickelodean*, with thee.
To where? I do not know nor care
as long as I'm with you.

Now, I must come to terms with my age and my ability to sail safely. My boat always offers me solitude. She seduces me by softly and slowly moving on the water to show me that she is alive. She is lovingly secured to her moor by two strong lines that are twice locked to her chocks, lest a sudden jolt release her to the wild river's whims. She, and all that's within her, is mine. All the things for my comfort and safety are held in their places by her. She shields me not only from the rain, wind and sea, but from the world's demands upon me. Alone with her, I can forget, reflect, relax and be at rest. I am totally in love with my boat.

Chapter Two

It is four o' clock in the morning when I arrived at my boat, and she is tugging to be freed. But she will not be free, and neither will I, until her powerful engine throbs to life and held her steady in the currents while I drop the lines that have held her prisoner to her moor. We now move up-stream, past the other boats until well clear and with a turn, enter the river channel at a right angle. Encountering no other traffic, save an occasional fishing boat, we move along Joppa Flats toward a rising sun and were treated to a small taste of heaven. Even before the sun has reached the horizon, it has set the sky ablaze with all the colors of a rainbow, smeared across the sky, for a spectacular show, just for us. The gold of the rising sun over the blue-green waters of the morning sea is being reflected by hundreds of panes of window glass in the cabins of Plum Island. The sky color ranged from orchid through gray, to vermilion laced with gold. I sit in total silence as I watched. The silence interrupted only by the wave-slap on the side of *Nickelodean*s bow. This is paradise!

Some cars are already parked in the Salisbury State Park alongside the northern edge of the river with their headlights still on. This is the same spot I like to watch the sunrise from my car. One person waves to me as *Nickelodean* rounds number seven "toothpick" buoy, within seventy-five feet of the stone jetty, with a right turn toward the mouth of the river. Moments later, we plow through the surf, and we are in my love's domain. We are in the Atlantic Ocean.

I could never describe my relationship with the ocean. Nervous, excitement, daring, thrilling, beautiful, adventurous, teasing, challenging, dangerous, glorious, tranquil, soothing and forbidding are but a few that come to mind. Others include relaxing, intriguing, welcoming and even spiritual. She can be quiet or noisy. She can make you wish your loved ones were with you or cause you to thank God they are not. She can be any one of these things or many of them at the same time. She is as fickle as she pleases, and she changes her mind and mood at her whim, but I love her!

But today, I am not on tour; I a looking for answers. As I point *Nickelodean*'s bow straight out to sea, the peace and solitude that I find here are exactly what I need and desire. I am ready to do some serious thinking, and if my approaching old age and my sailing future are not serious, then nothing is! The auto-pilot is turned on for the first time, and I set it to hold an easterly course. Winds are southwesterly at about twenty knots, perfect for an easy sail. I trim the mains'l (main-sail) angle, set the draft (or camber depth) of the sail and adjust it to be the same all the way up the leading edge....that's adjusted with the traveler. Now, I adjust the heads'l (forward sail) with much the same requirements and the sail-handling is complete. Now, I concentrate on the "heel" (tilt) of the boat and the "helm" or amount the wheel is held against the wind. All done! But I must go through this ritual again and again, doing less to correct the settings each time until no more are needed. We are moving well, and I ease (loosen) the sheets (lines for sail control) to relax the tell-tales (wind angle/speed indicators) slightly, and we are cruising. *Nickelodean* hums throughout her hull when she is cruising. The wind blowing through her piano-wire tight stays (steel cables) sing, as would a harp. Music for my soul!

I smile even greater as I watch dolphins play in the shockwave ahead of the bow, happily slowing to my speed and keeping their "aqua-dynamic" bodies angled alongside and slightly in trail of the leader, as well as any Blue Angel Navy pilot could do. They actually show their happiness as they glide through the clear-blue waters. The auto-pilot's beeps have died away because it has stiffened to it's assigned heading and is not moving, just waiting for the boat to make the slightest variance, when it will spring into action and save the day. I feel the need for a hot cup of coffee and, after checking for other traffic, go below.

The comfort of heat in my stomach, be it food or drink, always makes me feel good. One of the greatest things in life is a good cup of hot coffee. In all the places in the world, day or night, when relaxing or in serious concentration, hot coffee helps. I guess that's about any time. My old sailing friend Chuck Neilsen used to bring a thermos of hot stew for these moments. He introduced me to sailing and taught me to sail more years ago than I care to remember. He was a design engineer for hospital equipment and also built the best sailboats in the country and built model aircraft to perfection. He was the best builder of anything I have ever encountered. His model aircraft were indistinguishable from the real ones in a photograph. My favorite of his creations were his International, one-design, racing sailboats. They were made of wood but were so smoothly crafted that you could not tell that they were not fiberglass unless you cut one. His boats were safe and fast with unlimited sail adjustments and even a rotating, airfoil shaped, aluminum mast. They were so stable that they completely eliminated my son's "surprise knockdown maneuver," to my extreme delight. Chuck was also my advisor and source of accurate information on the building, repairing, sailing and handling of sailboats. I have often wondered how one man could store so much information, to the accuracy that he did, when he didn't use that information every day.

Chapter Three

Chuck has since passed away, but I can still remember the smile that he always displayed when sailing. When his boat cooperated with him, that's the way he indicated so, he displayed his great smile. But for the boat that didn't cooperate, there came an immediate verbal warning of impending change of design, layout or rigging. He was the only true jack-of-all-trades that I ever met. In all the years that I knew him, I have never seen a problem that he couldn't solve superbly. He was the true mentor of all my sailing skills.

When asked a question, he would listen intently, and while resting his chin on his thumb with his forefinger alongside his cheek, he would say, "Well, let's see!" That was always the last of that problem. He would immediately explain the answer. I never knew of one item that we disagreed on. We liked and did the same things, and I miss him greatly.

I miss many of my friends that are not available to me any longer. Lately, I have lost many friends, one after the other, for various reasons. One in war, one to an industrial accident, one to a recreational and one to an automobile accident, many to medical reasons, a suicide and one to the worst reason possible, drugs. It makes me sad to know I have lost them but happy to have known all of them and for the memories they left me.

I have always tried to attach myself to up-beat people and have had to work, hard at times, to remain so myself. I need to share, within my life's circle, my love for Mother Nature. My somewhat pantheistic, Christian beliefs become entwined while remaining true to my circle and my God. I believe that God is everywhere and in everything and that God is love. Once, I was sailing far from shore when tiny wings deposited a wasp on my arm. In my surprise and knowing their disposition, I swiped at it but missed. Expressing disapproval of my actions, the wasp promptly stung me. Now, I outweighed this fellow by thousands of times with a body mass of equal superiority, but it stood up to me.

However, I could not bring myself to harm it. He was rather stupid for attacking the Supreme Commander of the only boat for miles around in this vast ocean, but he was very brave. I could not bring myself to harm it, especially so far away from the safety of land. I believe that what we cannot replace, we should try not to destroy, lest you find yourself someday explaining to God just why you found His Creation insignificant. Nature is not yours to command. You have dominion over your children but does that mean that you can harm them? I think not! In my opinion, our dominion over animals means the same thing. Remember that God promised man and beast that he would not destroy the earth again by flood. Did not God therefore speak to animals in making that promise or is the Bible wrong? He promised them! Would The Creator speak to them if they were insignificant or not capable of understanding? Again, I think not! Would a just God cause them to love and suffer pain, as they do, if they were not to share the rewards of heaven, also? His point and that is good enough for me.

Chapter Four

I often wonder what it's all about, anyway. Do I have it right? I'm old enough, educated enough and inquisitive enough to understand. Protestants, Catholics, Jews, Muslims…does anyone have the correct answers? I guess everyone thinks that they do. I will be first to tell you that sometimes I think I do, and sometimes, I question my feelings. I look at a whale and know that some people say that he doesn't have a soul! What is a soul, anyway? Are they doomed to rejection from our afterlife? I hope not! I look after *Nickelodean* and ease the genoa sheet a mite. The sea is as smooth as silk and winds are slackening some.

After my last sail, where will I be? Where did all my friends go? Will I ever see them again, and if I do, will I know them? The Book is interpreted as many ways as there are readers and rightly so, I guess. After all, if you think about it, there is no world without you, and there is nothing in the world without and except you. The individual is the only definitive part of the circle of life, the center. Some people take the rules literally unless they disagree with them and then are quick to interpret for me. Here, at least and at last, I am at peace with myself, my God and nature. I totally relax and close my mind to thought and listen with my heart to the soothing sounds of the wind and the sea, as I enjoy the massage of a warm sea-breeze upon my face.

A bang and a loud flutter cause my heart to pound rapidly on the inner lining of my chest. I am immediately sweating in an already wet environment. I am startled to find a heavily swelling sea, hissing at me with a hot and disorientating sea fog. The boat is stopped, and the auto-pilot is still engaged with the wheel but is offering no assistance or alarm. All electrical power has been lost! I hadn't meant to fall asleep. I wonder how long it has been since I drifted off!

It seems like late day, but in sea fog, I can't be sure. I go below and check circuit breakers, recycling them off and on again. I check the overhead lights and find that there is no electrical power anywhere. I can't even start the engine. It doesn't have manual start, and besides, it is tilted to the up position by electro-hydraulics. I'm stuck!

Where am I? Must be east of port, compass showing south but for how long? Returning to topsides, I manually disconnect the auto-pilot. There is no steering. The boat does not respond to helm. Luckily, there are no waves, just swells that I feel but can't see. It is very disconcerting, to say the least. The swells slip under my bow accompanied by the threatening hiss of a heavy fog. The air creates a low moaning sound passing through the rigging. Why do usually welcomed sounds now feel so alien? Perhaps they are the voices of the wind-gods talking to me, and I, being out of touch with the spirits of my forefathers, cannot understand.

Sea fog's soft caress brings with it an erasure of all thought. Thought pictures are removed from my present environment. Here is now, still and soft, with a slight panic feeling. I feel somewhat helpless, with a loss of reasoning outside of my range of sight. All that is life is contained within my sight. Everything outside my ring is hostile. The hiss of the fog, the rustle of the lufting sails and the rolling of the nearly invisible sea threatens me. The sound of a small wave slapping the bow is magnified a hundred fold. Visions of reflected light in the fog dance on swells and then are gone, leaving me to feel alone with the ghosts of the sea. Why does rigging moan even when air is stilled? Foggy visions fade in and out, laughing softly at my plight even as they go, as if they know the only way to shore.

Evening's dark has always brought restful thoughts. Even the roar of the surf on a summer day is sweet and the winds always play a melodious tune through *Nickelodean*'s stays but the quietness of a sea-fog can be deafening. These moaning sounds bring to my body a blood-cold chill tonight.

Chapter Five

Now, I need to get this boat under some kind of control and pull myself together. Have to hold on to my senses! I have sailed in fog before, albeit not at night and not while I am lost. There's no helm and no air to set the sails to. I have to set some kind of course, somehow. I feel a swell and move the wheel back and forth as fast as I can to try turning down the backside of the swell. I tease myself that the boat is changing course. It reminds me of the "learning dam" that I was taught to avoid by my instructor in my flight instructor course at Fort Rucker, Alabama, a long time ago. (Gravity is a force that causes an item to fall - An object falls because of gravity.) The instructor would say, "You have led the student into a learning dam, sir! The student can learn nothing, and will be confused, from these true statements." I tell myself in my most commanding voice, *Well, guess what, Einstein. You can't get the boat to change course while dropping down a swell unless there's water passing over the rudder, sir!* But maybe gravity itself will rescue me. It works! *Nickelodean* changes her course, ever so slightly, each time she slides off a swell. But what course do I sail? Of course, I go for a westerly heading to take me back to the east coast. Seems like hours to make the compass swing to the new heading. But I can hear air passing through the stays. I still can't feel any movement or force from it, but I can hear a faint moaning from the upper rigging. It sure sounds good when you're desperately looking for air.

I remember from childhood, when I had a good place to hide from the world staked out in the warm sun to dream in, my mother would call to me with the sweet sound of a mother's voice. I must admit, however, that, at times, I didn't answer. Soon, she would stop calling. But now, I know that she knew where I was most of the time and would let me be, as I later would do with my children. I wish I could wake up from this nightmare and go home.

"Aaahhhh!" I scream. My boat shudders as she collides with something in the fog. I scream again, consciously and instinctively and as loud as I can. The crunching sound of a collision in a moving sea is repeated two, no, three times, and I close my eyes in a desperate act of survival and defense. I survey our lot! We had collided, but with what?

An ugly mixture of brown and green seawater colors the foam running down my deck. *Nickelodean* is being held around her forestay by some slimy monstrous thing. She needs help here and now. I gather all my being, and without further plan or thought, I rush forward to fight the tangled mess from her rig. I place my hand in the bulk and pull all that will give up its grasp off to one side. Then, another handful. *It's moving!* I think to myself. Another handful, then another, then it becomes easier. As I continue my chore, I begin to see the remainder of the object. "An old boat!" I say, talking directly to *Nickelodean*. "It's just an old boat! It must have surfaced by a storm after years at sea!"

I have heard of such happenings before, but this is my first encounter. I am so relieved! It is, or was, an old sailboat with a broken mast and a whole timber for a boom that is still wrapped with yellowy scraps of yard that was her sails. A long piece of some kind of yellowed line hung from her stem, which I quickly secured to *Nickelodean*'s aft, port chock. My boat has been hit. I return forward again to assess the damages but, except for a few pieces if slimy sticks and a few patches of old yard, there is little evidence of collision. "Well, now! That's a conversation piece to drag back to the yacht club!" I laugh at myself for panicking and remembered that a friend had collided with a picnic table, with seats for eight, some two miles from shore after the spring floods of '98.

Chapter Six

Nickelodean comes through again! The construction methods used by the Lancer Company to build the Power-sailor were superb. From the five-foot bow to the 150-horsepower engine meant to slam her through the rough Pacific coastal waters and everything in between. These are the strongest sailing vessels I have ever seen. *Nickelodean* is a motor-sailor and can sail at speeds comparable with pure sailboats her size and then run away from them under power. She's a tough sweetheart and a joy to sail, and I am so proud to own her.

As I walk to the cockpit, I can still hear the sound of the wind, but it has not lowered itself down the sails. Soft moans fade and re-appear. The old hulk that I retrieved is bumping *Nickelodean*'s stern, so I have decided to pull it alongside. I pulled the slimy mass along, by pulling the old bow line under the lifelines and then secured it to *Nickelodean*'s forward mooring chock. With closer scrutiny, I notice that it is the remains of an old fisherman's dinghy. Another old line, perhaps used as a mainsheet, hangs from the aft end of the boom. The stem, or bow, was desperately trying to move away from *Nickelodean*'s side, and to speed the lashing process, I pulled rather hard on this line while making it fast to the forward chock.

"Aaiieeee!" The old yards flew into the air as great pain engulfed my hand. I don't understand what is happening! Even the noise is confusing as I am not screaming. I am in silent shock as a rusty object has pierced my hand completely, and in reaction to my agony, I pulled it away and lifted my hand free, placing it in the other for protection.

I shake uncontrollably as an object the shape of a man climbs screaming and slashing onto my boat. "Lay away now, else a' hl feed yer guts t' th' sharks!" it yelled. "Who ye be, n' what 'av ye done with muh boat?" He continues yelling.

"E sent ye, didn't 'e? Now, yuv foun' me, move t' the gunnels n' face the sea! A' hl find who y' are. What this raft be?"

The cut is bleeding heavily, and I plead with this old wisp to let me wrap my hand. He seems too busy looking at my boat to object, so I wrapped my hand in my t-shirt. I don't now how this thing can live. He has no flesh, just skin over bone. He seems unsure of his surroundings and is hungry, I'm sure. I move down the stairs to the galley, and before he can object, I meet his advance with a loaf of bread. He is in total confusion, as I am, and I wonder if I have unwittingly played my trump card of food too early. I offered the food with the only hand I had left to defend myself with. He hesitated but not for long and, holding the loaf with both hands, tore away large chunks with his toothless mouth and swallowed it directly with very little movement of his skeletal jaws. I quickly offered water and more food, and he began to calm down somewhat. I could see his dark eyes deeply recessed in his head, darting about as he ate like a wild animal, torn between his food and his captive cage. He still holds the rusty knife at the ready, and I am shaking uncontrollably.

Chapter Seven

"Who are you?" I ask in the calmest voice that I could muster under the circumstances.

"Ne'er ye mind what name is mine. E sent ye, didn't 'e? A' hl ne'er go back n' run thu gauntlet o' death, not me, mate, not old Bones. Yu'l ne'er see thu Witch. What this raft be?"

"I don't understand you!" I plead. "Let's sit and talk a while. This is my sailboat, and this is the engine that pushes her along when the wind is not fair!" I realize that I haven't been basic enough. He can't possibly understand what an engine and fiberglass is, coming from that era. "Now, wait a minute!" I snap loudly. What am I doing? Oh well, I have to go along with this charade or whoever is pulling this trick will have the laugh on me.

Silence held the air full still while the old man seemed to take it all in or, at least, to take a big gulp. He says, "Ne'er ye mind ye make old Bones thu fool, war ye hail?"

"Newburyport, Massachusetts, sir, and you?" I ask sarcastically. The knife flies past my ear so closely that I could feel the wind. I grabbed and suddenly was lying on top of this snarling, smelly mass of bones. I wrestle the rusty knife from his feeble grip and throw it overboard. Holding him immobile with my weight, I demand his cooperation. He slowly gets up on his feet and, for a while, stands in a surrendered silence. We eat, drink and talk, sometimes in a language that neither he nor I could understand, but through determination, signs and a "professional" understanding of marine needs, slowly began to converse.

He tells me that he was born in the Shetlands, didn't know when, named Jonathan and was bartered by his father to work aboard the ship *Black Witch* as a cabin boy, to a captain, name of Conant. The first mate, called Silverbeard, commandeered the ship, killing Conant. After attending a meeting in Jamaica in 1720 with two women pirates, name of Anne Bonny and Mary Reed, Silverbeard took the *Black Witch* and sea-wolfed the east coast of America from Jamaica to the Isles of Shoals off the Massachusetts coast. Two years earlier in 1718, Silverbeard's brother, Blackbeard, actually Edward Teach, had been killed by the commander of the British Navy's *HMS Pearl*, and his head attached to the bowsprit of the *Pearl* as it navigated the James River in Virginia. Silverbeard and another pirate, name of Roberts, had shared a harborage in the Isles of Shoals, with the cooperation of the Massachusetts governor, and no others dared to venture there. Sailors who became too old, sick or weak were left there to labor to their death while building catches of stone for their bounties.

Being a passing student of maritime history, I realize that the names, dates and events in his stories were essentially accurate. *Is this the biggest joke on me, or what?* I think.

How is it being played, by whom and for what reason? How does this old man know so much history, and where did they find him, and how did they get us together in this fog? Why make him do this? He is so frail. All this time the old man rattled on, spilling his thoughts now, as if I can save him from whatever he fears so much.

"Where did you find that old boat?" I interrupt, trying to catch him off guard. He curses me and raises his tightly wrapped bones to support his other hand in its undefined endeavors. I can't allow myself to be distracted any more, and I slide *Nickelodean* off a swell, picking up a hope of speed.

He tells of treaties that were honored by diplomats and thieves alike. He tells me of Captain John Avery, who had commandeered a Mogul's ship, containing 10,000 pieces of eight, along with the Mogul's daughter and had bribed the Massachusetts governor to dispose of his plunder. I know this to be true, but *I wonder, How did he know this information and more importantly, why?* He continues on.

Chapter Eight

First, they had relieved Spanish galleons of their cargo, then any ship of their gold. Usually, no prisoners were taken. Young, able bodied men were offered a choice of joining the pirating crew or to be forced to work as laborers at the Isles of Shoals. The older captive crewmen and the infirm were summarily killed. Later, anyone who got to be feeble, weaker or disobeyed, was sentenced to run the gauntlet of death at a day's edge.

"What is this gauntlet of death and just what is a day's edge?" I ask.

He tells me that Silverbeard had lost and arm to infection after a battle wound. His replacement arm had been made for him during a visit to Jamaica, with a knife where the hook would have been, and the length of the arm increased by one span. Sailors who were too old to be useful or were condemned to die for dereliction of their duties were shackled and brought to stand on the ships gunnels when one days sail, called a day's edge from shore fall.

Silverbeard would slit their throats with his arm's knife as all the crew was forced to watch and pushed them overboard to the sharks. No one could outreach Silverbeard's arm to defend himself. This old man had known that his time had come and had stolen a boat and disappeared in the foggy darkness.

He went on to tell me that he couldn't remember when he got the name "Bones," but it seemed as if he had always had it. He hadn't been called Jonathan since he last saw his father. He argues with me over and over again that the place I call Maine, toward which I keep trying to steer, did not exist, and that caused him to be suspicious of me. I think that my insistence that it indeed did exist only made him more nervous. He argues that only the Isles of Shoals and Massachusetts lie to our west.

Defenses are beginning to relax. The fog is still dense, but it is good to not hear the moaning.

"What's yer lot? War ye bound? Why 'av ye come fer me? Why 'elp 'im?" The old man's questions seem to go on forever.

"Wait, hold on! I told you before that I am from Newburyport, Massachusetts. I fell asleep, and when I awoke, I was hopelessly lost in this fog. I don't know who this 'E' is, and I am helping no one, even myself, at this moment!" I try again to explain. "I feel that we are a day or so north and east of the Isles of Shoals, and if we sail west, we'll find the coast of Maine." It feels good to talk, even if I am not getting through to him and I go on. "I also feel the threat of aging, not to the extent of the story that you have concocted, but nonetheless, it is having an effect on my being! I would think that you are an image of this fog and my mind, but you have given me actual pain. I should throw you back into that wreck and shove you back to hell!"

He winches, as if struck by lightning, and tore the magnetic compass from its mounting and threw it into the water, all before I could react.

"What are you doing, you fool?' I yell at him.

"Yer 'ere t' elp 'im ah know, ye wretch, war ye goin' now?" He laughs. His laugh reminded me of a laughing gulls yelp.

"Well, I was trying for the Massachusetts or Maine coastline, but I'll never find them now, you've seen to that!"

"A' ve done ye a mighty favor, matey! A' ve tol' ye 'eres no Maine and the Isles, well, ne'er go near, or yu'l die fer sure!"

We both fall silent at the same moment that a breath of air was sensed, ever so lightly, but air, moving air. I wet my ears and move my head to balance the coolness to determine the wind direction. I face the wind; it's there, slightly off the stern to starb'd! Confidence returns quickly as *Nickelodean* leaves a ripple and bubbles, ever so slightly in the still, smooth waters. "Help me work the wind!" I thought that a sailor, even when he's lying, is still a sailor. It worked! When the tell-tales would move, even slightly, I shout out with glee, "We're moving! I don't know what direction but we're moving!"

After a few minutes of making headway, the old man stands abruptly and freezes, as if paralyzed.

"What's the matter?" I ask.

"It's th' gold!" he says. "I took th' sack o' gold and ran away!"

"Where is this gold?" I ask.

"In th' boat!" He searches the wreck and came up with no trace of any bag. "Silverbeard 'ul kill me fer sure!" he says.

"You lying old man, you told me a while ago that you were marked for death because of your age anyway, so why would you care about gold, if there ever was any? It seems that you are in a damned if you do and damned if you don't situation!" I cut it short, seeing from his face that he didn't appreciate my humor. However, I add, "We are in the same boat, in more ways than one, old fella!" My conversation has turned to giddiness in my excitement.

Chapter Nine

"You still haven't told me who this E is. Who is he?" I ask.

"E is 'im, Silverbeard, that's who!" he yelps.

We work together now, looking for a whisper of air. First here, then there, it moves around but we are moving. It's happening! Hours go by, and a quiet darkness has set in again. I am still trying to sort this all out in my mind, which was already hurting for space, when this noise, ever so slightly breaks the silence of the fog. First comes disbelief, then we listen intently. I hear another noise that is slightly musical. Then, I definitely hear a voice, then laughter, then the unmistakable sound of hooves on lumber, horses on a dock. Smiling, I stand silently, in frozen anticipation.

Through the fog, a dark object appears. A ship, a ship at a dock. "It's a tall ship!" I yell as loud as my voice would let me.

Then, someone on the docks pointed at me and yells to another, "What is that boat doing here?"

Before I can ease the genoa, the old man yells, "I shudda slit yer throat w'en I had thu chance, yuh wretch! Ye are with 'im!" And with that, he jumps into his relic and disappears into the foggy bay. I release the genoa sheet and spin full rudder towards the docks, and *Nickelodean* comes about a full 180 degrees, I judge. I notice, for the first time, that the wind had freshened and shifted, and the boat is reacting nicely. *I think, I'll follow the docks to a place where I can tie up and ask directions; perhaps buy a new compass and get the electrical system and the engine back.* I trim the sails and look again for the docks that I now have lost in the darkness. The dock, the shoreline, anything, I don't want to lose it, but after many turns with no compass, I have lost all sight and sounds of whatever I saw.

Suddenly, the keel slams into a rock heavy shudders come from within the bowels of my boat as she slides off to lee and is again rocked by collision. But I have eased sails, and she is at least holding headway speed. Turning to port, I battle to keep her bow perpendicular to the waves then 45 degrees from the unseen, but noisy surf that we have been thrust into. I can only guess and hope that the bow is pointed toward where the last wave came from. I can't let the helm free for a moment or she'll broach for sure. With my hand continuously on the wheel, she seems to have relaxed after a while and I realized that we are back in blue water. I am devastated that we were so close and, now, so far away from the shore.

It is soon daylight again, and I am still hopelessly lost in a dense fog with no compass, no power and no electricity. Even if I had a compass, I ask myself, *What direction would I go, where have I been and what does my family think?* I begin to worry about my family for the first time. They know my procedure, "If the river mouth is too rough to come in to, I would sail in deep water until the fog dissipates or the ocean calmed down." But how long have I been gone and has the water been rough at the river entrance? Is it foggy where they are, well inland?

My hand has stopped bleeding, and I bathe it often in sea water. I have been keeping the slight glow from the rising sun, above the fog, to my back. That should keep me headed westerly. I hope my wound is not infected from that rust. I find that my knee and back are in constant pain, and I am extremely weary. *Nickelodean* is excellent for holding her course when her sails are trimmed properly, and now, I can close my eyes. It feels good! I know I shouldn't chance falling to sleep, but I am very tired, and I will just rest them for a few seconds. I am so very tired.

I am startled as I am awakened by the audible alarm of the auto-pilot's *beep-beep-beep*. Sweeter sounds were never heard. The electrical power is back. It is dark again. I must have slept for several hours. Some lights are on. I don't know what happened, but they are back on. The radar is back, along with the digital compass on the auto-helm auto-pilot. "Oh Glory, I can start the engine!" I wonder if the ignition is too wet. "Please don't be wet!" The big engine lowers into the water and roars to life at the first touch of the starter switch. I am on my way west toward home, home from this nightmarish madness. Best power is set at 75% throttle, and I have enough fuel for seven and a half hours of engine run time, if I force myself not to hurry. That will take a lot of discipline. "Let's go home, Nick!"

The GPS showed the direction and the distance to the #2 buoy in the Merrimack River entrance channel. No traffic is observed on the radar. Once I am at the buoy, I change to #7 toothpick buoy and enter the channel between the north and south jetties. After radar shows me the way around #7 buoy, I take up a heading of 278 degrees, and we are rolling home. "Yahoo!" I yell at no one in particular. We slow to approach Half-tide Rocks and, alongside, turn toward the American Yacht Clubs mooring field, but I think, *I will moor her in the morning,* and secure the chock lines to the docks.

I secure the engine and stretch out, for the first time, with a big pillow on *Nickelodean*'s soft, queen-size bunks.

Chapter Ten

"Aaiieee! Ye poor excuse fer shark food. On yer feet! Steal the gold and run away, will ye!" someone is growling. The old man was standing above me, shattering my sleep and laughing in that sea-gull sound and saying, "Tol' ye I'd fetch 'im cap'n. E's thu one 'at did it! Old Bones foun' yer gold fer ye an' I 'av it 'ere!"

He held out a small bag to the man with the silver beard and the wooden arm. I am immediately placed in shackles, shackles that I have seen many times before. Two strong sailors lift me up to the gunnels, and I felt hot pain sear my throat as I, life fading quickly, fell into the bloody waters below. It is October 1, 1723.

The Final Chapter

August 24, 2004

The Newburyport Harbor master, towing a blood covered boat to police impoundment at the Windward Yacht Yard, does not notice a small, yellowed piece of line that drops from the forward chock into the waters and floats towards shore. As the boat is pulled from the water, an old man and a young lady watch. The young girl picks up the old piece of line and walks toward her grandfather. Life goes on.

ABOUT THE AUTHOR

C.D. Hurley grew up around (and often in) Cherokee Lake, in the Five Rivers area of the rolling hills of East Tennessee that are often referred to as "The Highlands of Dixie." Nestled between the Cumberland and Great Smoky Mountains, these beautiful surroundings lent greatly to molding the mind of this young man.

His prior release, *REVERIE—A Kaleidoscope of the Prose and Poetry in My Life* (PublishAmerica), exhibited his first works. In this second collection of prose and poetry, he has added, for your enjoyment, a sea story. So, come along again and re-dream our yesterdays in this *POT O' GOLD*.

Author's Note:

I was always told of the POT O' GOLD at the end of the rainbow and had to live a lifetime before I realized that, all along, I had found it!

Printed in the United States
34330LVS00006B/22-69

9 781413 779080